To my own little t-Rex ~

Curious Little T-Rex
First published by Art by Chia in 2021.
Wellington, New Zealand
Text © Chia Rubio
Illustrations © Chia Rubio

Format: Softcover - POD
ISBN: 978-0-473-59691-0
Publication Date: 11/2021

Format: E-pub
ISBN: 978-0-473-59692-7
Publication Date: 11/2021

artbychia@gmail.com

Curious Little T-Rex

Story and Illustrations
by Chia Rubio

•

Art by Chia

It was a nice sunny
day outside. Daddy
T-Rex, Mama T-Rex
and Little T-Rex
just finished their
breakfast.

"What do you want to
do today Little T-Rex?"
asked Mama T-Rex.

"Let's go exploring!"

he said brightly.

"Exploring? Alright, let's take a walk and see what we can find." Daddy T-Rex smiled.

The dinosaur family went out and decided to go in the forest and head on a path they haven't taken before. "This is exciting isn't it..."

'Wait, what's that?"
said curious Little T-Rex unexpectedly as he suddenly SAW something.
Little T-Rex thought it was like a house with a red broad roof covered with spots on top of a long pillar.

"It's a mushroom!" said Mama T-Rex.
"Cool! Interesting, I thought mushrooms are only supposed to be tiny and brown..."

Curious Little T-Rex stopped as he SMELLED something.

He thought it was fragrant, it smells fresh and minty.

"Those are mint leaves!" Mama T-Rex said.
"Cool! Interesting, maybe we can use it in our food sometime."

They picked a few mint leaves but he also picked something else and tried to TASTE it.

"Wait, what's this?"

Curious Little T-Rex thought it was sweet but a little tart.

"Hmm, those are raspberries!" said Daddy T-Rex.
"Cool! Interesting, I only had blueberries but these ones are really good too." He ate some more and continued walking.

"Wait, what's that?"
Curious Little T-Rex tilted his head as he HEARD something.

He thought it sounded like a gentle roar —
a loud splashing sound but very soothing.

"It's a waterfall!" Daddy T-Rex pointed. "Cool! Interesting, can we take a dip?"
The dinosaur family excitedly jumped in the water.

"Wait, what's that?"

Curious Little T-Rex FELT something brushed his leg while swimming.

He thought it was soft and maybe a bit slimy.

"Oh, it's seaweed!" as Mama T-Rex looked under the water.
"Cool! Interesting, there are also plants underwater, so
green and leafy..."

"Are you having fun today?"
Daddy asked.
"Yes, so much fun exploring,
especially with you, Daddy
and Mama T-Rex!"

The
dinosaur
family went
home after
their fun
exploration.

They were
all tired
but happy
with their
adventure
and new
discoveries
together.

"Wait, what's that?"

Find more about the author/illustrator
Instagram: @artbychia
Facebook: @artbychia
Email: artbychia@gmail.com

Think and Create ~